# 1001
## SEX SECRETS
## EVERY WOMAN
## SHOULD KNOW

D0833244

# 1001

## SEX SECRETS
## EVERY WOMAN
## SHOULD KNOW

### Researched by
### CHRIS ALLEN

AVON BOOKS NEW YORK

AVON BOOKS
A division of
The Hearst Corporation
1350 Avenue of the Americas
New York, New York 10019

Library of Congress Cataloging in Publication Data:
Allen, Chris. 1963-
  1001 sex secrets every woman should know / researched by Chris Allen.
    p.   cm.
1. Sex—Miscellanea. 2. Men—Sexual behavior—Miscellanea. I. Title. II. Title: One thousand one sex secrets every woman should know. III. Title: One thousand and one sex secrets every woman should know.
HQ23.A426        1993                                      94-32316
306.7—dc20                                                 CIP

First Avon Books Trade Printing: February 1995

AVON TRADEMARK REG. U.S. PAT. OFF. AND IN OTHER COUNTRIES, MARCA REGISTRADA, HECHO EN U.S.A.

Printed in the U.S.A.

OPM 10 9 8 7 6 5 4 3

# <u>Preface</u>

The following material was obtained over a period of eleven months. The participants were selected at random. Responses were gathered through face-to-face conversations, telephone replies and written surveys. Men were given the opportunity to volunteer their thoughts independently, as well as complete sentences such as: "I love it when...," "The one thing I wish my wife/girlfriend/all women knew about sex is...," "The best sex I ever had was..." and so on. Please be aware that this project was not designed to be a psychological, sociological or clinical study, nor was it intended to serve as an accurate representation of the entire male population. The only thing it was ever meant to be was REAL.

# 1001

## SEX SECRETS
## EVERY WOMAN
## SHOULD KNOW

**1.**

A little variety goes a long way.

*--Charles, 32*

**2.**

Never schedule lovemaking. It's much more fun to play it by ear.

*--Danny, 29*

**3.**

I resent it when she gives me the third degree.

*--Matt, 35*

**4.**_____

Fellatio is the most valuable
weapon in her sexual arsenal.

*--Ken, 24*

**5.**_____

Most women have three or four
"man-catching" moves and that's it.
Show me there's something more.

*--Marty, 30*

**6.**_____

I like a woman who can let the
animal inside her take over in bed.

*--Paul, 27*

_____

_____ _**7.**

You don't need to trash my old
girlfriends to build yourself up.

       *--Peter, 22*

_____**8.**

I love it when she lets out this
little squeal of pleasure.

       *--Anthony, 28*

_____**9.**

Stop punishing me for what other
guys have done to you.

       *--Bobby, 31*

_____

## 10.

It's not only how you feel about your partner, it's how you feel about yourself when you're with them.

*--Alan, 28*

## 11.

Your women friends exaggerate their sexual experiences just as much as my men friends.

*--Chris, 31*

## 12.

Compromise is the key.

*--George, 44*

**13.**

Don't be afraid to tell me what you like.

*--John, 30*

**14.**

It's not a conscious decision.  My body really does want to shut down and sleep after sex.

*--Kyle, 23*

**15.**

The world's biggest turn-off is feeling sorry for yourself.

*--Preston, 26*

## 16.

My girlfriend and I try to come up with different "delights" at least once a week.

*--Neil, 27*

## 17.

I know you don't want intercourse when you're on your period, but some fellatio would certainly make the week go by faster.

*--David, 31*

## 18.

Nagging wives make lousy lovers.

*--Keith, 36*

**19.**

Most women don't need alcohol to feel less inhibited. It's simply an excuse to do what they really want.

*--Larry, 25*

**20.**

I love to make her laugh in bed.

*--Michael, 33*

**21.**

I wish women knew that we can't choose to have an erection (or choose not to have one).

*--Jamie, 28*

## 22.

When you climax, don't be afraid to make some noise.

*--Tom, 38*

## 23.

When it's obvious you're tired of giving me oral sex, there's no way I'm going to come.

*--Mark, 32*

## 24.

The woman you're constantly comparing yourself to doesn't exist. *You* do. And you're beautiful.

*--Ben, 24*

**25.**

I wish she could talk about her body without being embarrassed.

*--Glenn, 28*

**26.**

An all-over body massage says "I love you" more than sex.

*--Erik, 27*

**27.**

You can have multiple orgasms, whereas I can only have one. Make sure it's the best one I can have.

*--Lenny, 35*

## 28.

If she insists on talking through it all, it better be directly related to the sex we're having.

*--Kurt, 29*

## 29.

Whenever she buys lingerie or panties she always models them for me that night.

*--James, 37*

## 30.

I like your basic red lips and shiny, black stilettos.

*--Russ, 31*

**31.**

Forget those TV ads.  Women are sexiest when they sweat.

--*Steve, 31*

**32.**

I know when she wants to make love because those legs of hers are always smooth.

--*Robert, 39*

**33.**

I'm going to be as rough as you'll let me.  It's up to you to tell me when to ease up.

--*Sean, 29*

**34.**_____

Sexy underwear makes any woman's body more desirable.

*--Jeff, 21*

**35.**_____

Always keep a couple of big, clean blankets in the trunk in case the urge hits the two of you on the road.

*--Richard, 46*

**36.**_____

Women aren't the only ones who like to be pampered.

*--Jim, 34*

_____

_____**37.**

Let's do it in the morning more often.

*--Alex, 30*

_____**38.**

If you're not in the mood, say so. Excuses bite.

*--Todd, 22*

_____**39.**

When I offer to buy you a drink, I'm being hospitable--not trying to get you drunk so I can do you.

*--Bud, 29*

_____

## 40._____

I love to watch her give me oral
sex.

*--Billy, 25*

## 41._____

Your skin is never softer than when
you come out of the shower.

*--Ed, 34*

## 42._____

My ex-girlfriend never wanted to
try anything new. You don't want
to have even your favorite food
every night, do you?

*--Frank, 27*

_____

**43.**

If I haven't made the first move in awhile, it means I'd like you to.

*--Joe, 30*

**44.**

I prefer women who can appreciate the little things as well as the "biggies."

*--Christopher, 26*

**45.**

If we're using an unlubricated condom, put it on me with your mouth.

*--Rob, 23*

## 46.

If my wife could be a man for just one night, I think she'd understand the sexual pressure I feel from her.

*--Jim, 38*

## 47.

Don't wait until we're done to tell me how close you were to an orgasm.

*--Gene, 32*

## 48.

I love it when she wears things she knows I like.

*--Lee, 27*

**49.**

A back rub feels almost as good as a "front rub."

*--Victor, 29*

**50.**

Give me sex as often as you can stand it.

*--Tim, 32*

**51.**

After about fifteen minutes of giving you cunnilingus, my jaw muscles are shot for the night.

*--Wayne, 24*

## 52.

My wife and I always try to do it twice in one evening. First, it's a quick one for me. Then I can take my time and make her feel good.

*--Warren, 37*

## 53.

I love a woman that curses like a sailor while we're doing it.

*--Lewis, 31*

## 54.

I love the feel of her hair on my shoulder after we've made love.

*--Leonard, 38*

**55.**

If you're going to do something new in bed, don't tell me, just do it.

*--Doug, 28*

**56.**

My lady is constantly using her hands all over me no matter what she's doing with the rest of her body.

*--Elliott, 31*

**57.**

I tune everything out during sex, including you. Talk to me after.

*--Walt, 30*

**58.**_____

No more complaints about your looks. I think you're beautiful, and that should count for something.

*--Carl, 28*

**59.**_____

Unless you tell me some things that you like, I'm going to do exactly what I like and that's all.

*--Nick, 31*

**60.**_____

Sometimes we just lay together nude, side by side, touching.

*--Chad, 43*

_____

## 61.

Instead of applying pressure on the downstroke of my penis, do it on the upstroke.

*--Bob, 24*

## 62.

I guess the pressure they put on us to perform is payback for our pressure on them to put out.

*--Jay, 23*

## 63.

I love it when we change positions with me still inside her.

*--Mark, 32*

**64.**_____

My wife and I buy each other
unusual underwear. Different
clothes inspire different thoughts.

*--Bill, 33*

**65.**_____

One of the big reasons I love my
wife is that I know if we see
something kinky in a movie, I'm
going to get to try it later.

*--Craig, 30*

**66.**_____

Sex and love are apples and oranges.

*--Harvey, 26*

_____

_____**67.**

I really don't want to do it when your having your period, no matter what your hormones say.

*--Mike, 28*

_____**68.**

I prefer older, more experienced women.  Young ones are too rough.

*--Alan, 23*

_____**69.**

I don't give damn if you queef.

*--Lou, 35*

_____

## 70._____

My wife and I always go into the kitchen after we make love for a post-orgasmic smorgasbord.

*--Evan, 28*

## 71._____

She begins oral sex by starting at my ankles and working her way up.

*--Thomas, 32*

## 72._____

Every good quality you exhibit in bed cancels out ten bad ones in all other areas combined.

*--Stephen, 32*

**73.**

The muscles in my shoulders must be connected to my penis.  When they're relaxed, it is, too.

*--John, 34*

**74.**

She gives me a massage when I come home from work.  It's the next best thing to sex.

*--Daniel, 45*

**75.**

Sex is best when she's the one that starts it.

*--Darryl, 32*

## 76.

Cap off the entire lovemaking experience by sharing a brandy or fine liqueur.

*--Josh, 37*

## 77.

Tell me your favorite cologne or after-shave and I'll be wearing it the next day.

*--Rob, 38*

## 78.

I'm always attracted to women who appreciates the value of money.

*--John, 41*

## 79.

I have a general idea of what feels
good, but it always helps to be told
exactly what you like.

*--Scott, 38*

## 80.

Good looks are a definite turn-on,
but I'm also aroused by a sense of
humor, intelligence, and sweetness.

*--Rusty, 40*

## 81.

If you're great in bed I couldn't
care less about your cooking skills.

*--Ray, 31*

## 82.

Men wouldn't be inclined to go to sleep immediately after sex if you began your day by making love instead of ending with it.

*--Stan, 43*

## 83.

Changing positions frequently is a good way to avoid the wet spot.

*--Ted, 29*

## 84.

Soft lighting and dim lighting are often confused.  Soft is best for sex.

*--Wes, 30*

**85.**

Once, my girlfriend gave me a hand job on a roller coaster.

*--Mark, 24*

**86.**

I always thought my married friends were full of it, but now that I am in love, I must admit it *does* improve the quality of our sex.

*--Joseph, 33*

**87.**

Put on a strip show and let me stuff dollar bills down your G-string.

*--Stu, 27*

## 88._____

I love to catch her sneaking a peek
at my crotch.  Sometimes I think she
knows that and lets me catch her.

*--Graham, 36*

## 89._____

Massage me without ever touching
my genitals.

*--Jon, 33*

## 90._____

You can keep me from coming by
tightly squeezing your hand around
the base of my penis.

*--Rick, 29*

**91.**

My favorite position is when I'm on my knees and she's on her side.

*--Jerry, 25*

**92.**

I like to get a little rough right before I come.

*--Gregg, 27*

**93.**

Call me into the kitchen with your nightie hiked up, bent over the counter. It's crude, but effective.

*--Jeffrey, 32*

## 94.

Long nails may look nice, but they sure can be painful.

*--Andrew, 30*

## 95.

Underwater intercourse--there is no substitute.

*--Brandon, 21*

## 96.

It's interesting watching adult videos with a woman. If it doesn't make her uncomfortable, she really provides a unique perspective.

*--Brad, 41*

**97.**

We have our porch swing set at the perfect height to where I can be standing and rock her back and forth, in and out.

*--Charlie, 39*

**98.**

If I bring a woman home for the night, it's not a marriage proposal.

*--Cliff, 32*

**99.**

Tell me up front if you're not going to swallow.

*--Mike, 23*

## 100.

Skinny girls aren't nearly as nice in bed as the big ones. Who wants to snuggle up to a bag of bones?

*--Marvin, 38*

## 101.

I wish she was half as concerned with pleasing me as she is with her clients at work.

*--William, 48*

## 102.

I highly recommend second honeymoons.

*--Jack, 59*

## 103.

For the last time; I'm not looking for my mother.

*--Tony, 31*

## 104.

No girl is ever gonna tie me up.

*--Roger, 24*

## 105.

If you've already got kids, don't expect me to be an instant father.

*--Steven, 29*

## 106.

I won't have sex without a condom.
It doesn't feel as good, but it feels
better than being dead.

*--Kirk, 25*

## 107.

I'm not going to get an immediate
erection every time you brush
against me.

*--Ron, 32*

## 108.

Beautiful girls are a delight, but
those with heart are true treasures.

*--Steve, 45*

## 109.

If you act sexy and attractive, you *are* sexy and attractive.

*--Allan, 37*

## 110.

I hope those ribs and things they put on condoms give her some pleasure, because they don't do a damn thing for me.

*--Rich, 31*

## 111.

A little mystery is fine when we're dating, but in bed I want to know.

*--Nathan, 29*

## 112.

I like that my wife always smells fresh and clean, not perfumed.

*--Mickey, 37*

## 113.

The ultimate was when she showed up at my office and did me under the desk.

*--Ned, 34*

## 114.

Ask yourself how important sex is in the success of your relationship, then choose your mate accordingly .

*--Henry, 42*

_____**115.**

My favorite sexual memory was
when I woke up to her giving me
fellatio.

*--Hank, 30*

_____**116.**

I'm not in this relationship because
I feel the need to perform for you.
I want the passion without the
pressure.

*--Grady, 34*

_____**117.**

No teeth.

*--Rick, 21*

_____

## 118.

The old "lady in the living room, chef in the kitchen, hooker in the bedroom" saying is as true as ever.

*--James, 38*

## 119.

We can talk all you want when we're not in bed. When we are, use your mouth in other ways.

*--Edward, 30*

## 120.

For a good laugh, you be me and I'll be you. Now try and seduce me.

*--Lenny, 27*

**121.**

Respect is earned, not given.  And that includes respecting you in the morning.

*--Phillip, 39*

**122.**

If I can satisfy her, it's almost as good as my orgasm.

*--Harry, 34*

**123.**

Don't ask me how you rate compared with other women.

*--Del, 42*

## 124.

Women who understand the give
and take involved in dancing
together are always the best in bed.

*--Bo, 28*

## 125.

The skin on the bottom of my penis
is the most sensitive.

*--Mark, 30*

## 126.

I have a weakness for women who
can knead the tension out of my
shoulders.

*--Andy, 34*

## 127.

Sometimes when we're driving home, my girlfriend will get in the back seat and whisper in my ear all the things she wants me to do to her.

*--Max, 24*

## 128.

Where doesn't matter as long as it's with you.

*--Robert, 31*

## 129.

I think Will Rogers said it best: "I never had an orgasm I didn't like."

*--Hal, 42*

## 130.

We arrange sleep-overs for the kids at my wife's parents' house. Then we're free to do things that would give my in-laws heart attacks.

*--Paul, 36*

## 131.

I never want to have an orgasm until you've had one first.

*--Kenny, 28*

## 132.

Your breasts feel best when you put my hand there.

*--Howard, 32*

## 133.

Don't ever get a tattoo.

*--Terrence, 36*

## 134.

You don't have to be double-jointed to try a new position.  Use your imagination. You'll surprise your man and yourself.

*--Ray,  31*

## 135.

Leave your jewelry on sometimes.

*--Reg,  28*

## 136.

Stockings with garters may not be as convenient, but they sure are a lot sexier than pantyhose.

*--Arnold, 30*

## 137.

Entering you from behind feels the most natural.

*--Kris, 24*

## 138.

I like to make the first move.

*--Shawn, 22*

**_____139.**

I hate it when she flirts with other guys.

*--Rudy, 26*

**_____140.**

If you want to get my attention, you've got to show me some cleavage.

*--Gary, 25*

**_____141.**

Men love sex and plenty of it. Period.

*--Dan, 29*

## 142.

There's too much emphasis on
sexual technique.  Focus on *arousal*
technique and great sex is yours.

*--Burt, 38*

## 143.

I can't take a leak when I've got an
erection, so don't get mad if I get
out of bed when we're finished.

*--Neal, 28*

## 144.

I love it when she takes my hand
and leads me into the bedroom.

*--Vince, 35*

**145.**

When we're done, take the condom
off for me.

*--Luke, 23*

**146.**

There are no rules.

*--Timothy, 31*

**147.**

When you talk about what you like
or don't like you should be able to
talk in specifics.

*--Stuart, 36*

## 148.

Retaining that little girl quality is great as long as it doesn't include throwing a tantrum to get your way.

*--Mitch, 25*

## 149.

I don't expect a girl to give me some on the first date, but I do by the fifth.

*--Darren, 24*

## 150.

Think of me as your favorite charity and give generously and often.

*--Will, 32*

**151.**

We don't have to know each other that well before we do it. Having sex *is* getting to know me.

--*Rick, 28*

**152.**

Walk that line between pleasure and pain, just don't leave any scars.

--*Charles, 27*

**153.**

I believe everything a woman tells me when I'm horny, so be careful what you say.

--*Wayne, 25*

## 154.

We fill each other in on the events of our day first. That way we can tell who needs what the most.

*--Donald, 38*

## 155.

I'll tell you enough of my sexual history so you'll know I'm not a high risk, but the rest is private.

*--Barry, 27*

## 156.

Men see a woman as she sees herself.

*--Michael, 30*

## 157.

When you want me to come, tell me again and again and it will happen.

*--Gregory, 28*

## 158.

A little attitude is sexy on a woman.

*--Steven, 24*

## 159.

The best sex is always with her underneath me and the hot sun on my back.

*--Jimmy, 22*

# 160.

If you want to make sure you don't get pregnant, give me a reason to pull out before ejaculation.

*--Clay, 26*

# 161.

Lick my testicles and then blow on them.

*--Bruce, 29*

# 162.

Long hair brings a world of possibilities with it.

*--Lyle, 43*

## 163.

I love a bed that squeaks when we
do it.

*--Pat, 27*

## 164.

My penis is not breakable. Go ahead
and touch it.

*--Paul, 30*

## 165.

We know each other so well we
don't even have to ask if the other is
interested. I could only make love
to a woman I share a rapport with.

*--Glen, 34*

## 166._____

I love to have my calves and thighs rubbed.  Nothing relaxes me faster.

*--Bob, 38*

## 167._____

Getting drunk doesn't make you look better; it makes me more courageous.

*--Kip, 26*

## 168._____

Don't mother me, especially in the bedroom.

*--Chad, 24*

_____

**169.**

Press my face against your breasts.

*--David, 25*

**170.**

I like it fast and hard.

*--Eddie, 29*

**171.**

When I'm giving you cunnilingus,
try not to writhe around too much.

*--Kenneth, 28*

## 172.

I'm not interested in bizarre rituals involving chains, whips, or handcuffs.

*--John, 39*

## 173.

Always tell me when something feels good.

*--Peter, 32*

## 174.

There's nothing more satisfying than teaching a new lover what feels good.

*--Richard, 30*

_____**175.**

I have a couple of drinks
beforehand because it dulls my
senses and makes me last longer.

*--Joey, 26*

_____**176.**

Sex is the reason they call it "the
*great* outdoors."

*--Matthew, 23*

_____**177.**

I'll do whatever it takes to get you
to loosen up.

*--Brian, 27*

_____

## 178.

If I had pretended to know certain things about sex, I never would have learned them for real.

*--Don, 31*

## 179.

You shouldn't get jealous when I play with my dog.

*--Gerald, 28*

## 180.

The best way to let yourself go is to look at your lovemaking from an observer's point of view.

*--Jimmy, 56*

**181.**

Kneel down and slowly slide my underwear off.

*--Patrick, 29*

**182.**

I have a meter running in my head. When the tab for our date hits one hundred dollars, I think I should have simply gone to a prostitute.

*--Scott, 27*

**183.**

Leave your panties on and pull them to one side.

*--Craig, 33*

# 184.

I love the way she looks during sex when her hair gets all messed up.

*--Mike, 38*

# 185.

Make love blindfolded.

*--Chuck, 30*

# 186.

Wear those sexy stockings. And keep them on when we make love.

*--Steve, 35*

**187.**

Do what you normally do, but slow down.

*--Raymond, 32*

**188.**

When it's alright for me to come into the bathroom while she's on the toilet, I know we've hit a milestone in our relationship.

*--Victor, 29*

**189.**

When we're doggie-style, bring your ankles up against my thighs.

*--Jason, 25*

## 190.

Stay away from any man who won't let you get on top. They're control freaks.

*--Martin, 33*

## 191.

We're doing it standing up and I hold her left leg at the knee and bring it up to my arm pit.

*--Ken, 29*

## 192.

If you don't know I love you by now you're never going to know.

*--Steve, 30*

**193.**

I love it when we're just kissing and she reaches into my pants.

*--Eric, 32*

**194.**

It's not so much of an emotional thing for me as it is for her.

*--Greg, 29*

**195.**

The best surface to make love on is a pool table.

*--Randall, 36*

# 196.

Every now and then, pull the mattress down onto the floor.

*--Bobby, 36*

# 197.

She puts us in sexual situations where there's some danger of getting caught. It's great.

*--Tom, 30*

# 198.

My wife is genuinely interested in what I like in bed. That's all any man could ever ask for.

*--Mark, 37*

**199.**

Just because I look at a *Playboy* doesn't mean I'm not turned on by you.

*--Carl, 26*

**200.**

If you must complain, don't whine.

*--Bill, 35*

**201.**

It's easy to pick out the women who've learned everything they know about men from reading *Cosmopolitan*.

*--Laurence, 30*

## 202.

Foreplay can only arouse you as much as you'll let it.

*--Charles, 31*

## 203.

It's hard to be turned on by you when you make me feel like a bad provider.

*--Douglas, 39*

## 204.

You can do what you want, tie me up or whatever, as long as I can do the same to you.

*--Tommy, 28*

**205.**

For God's sake, stop putting
yourself down.

*--John, 41*

**206.**

Her willingness to try something
new is a turn-on even when we're
not experimenting.

*--Neil, 32*

**207.**

Put the condom on me.

*--Paul, 27*

# 208.

**Trying for that perfect lovemaking experience requires you to have expectations. Those turn into limitations. Just let it happen.**

*--Frank, 38*

# 209.

**Women need to know how sensitive a guy's testicles are.**

*--Roy, 26*

# 210.

**At dinner, in bed, or wherever, always look me in the eye.**

*--Trent, 34*

## 211.

I have no respect for women who grant or withhold sexual favors in an effort to get their way.

*--Jeff, 34*

## 212.

Wrap your arms and legs around me at the same time.

*--Henry, 30*

## 213.

My facial expression does *not* change during nude scenes in movies no matter what you say.

*--Nate, 26*

## 214.

Most women are more beautiful than they think they are.

--*Jonathan, 31*

## 215.

During fellatio, make a circle with your thumb and forefinger and slide it up and down, too.

--*Mike, 28*

## 216.

Chinese food in bed, especially using chopsticks, is very sexy and romantic.

--*Gary, 27*

## 217.

Have you tasted your make-up lately?  Don't expect me all over you when you've got it on.

*--William, 26*

## 218.

Don't cultivate this "bad girl" image if you can't continue it in bed.

*--Eric, 27*

## 219.

You're great with my penis, now how about the rest of my body.

*--Sean, 30*

**220.**_____

Sexual gratification is only part of
the overall feeling of being taken
care of.

*--Jerry, 34*

**221.**_____

Oral sex with an ice cube in your
mouth.

*--Tom, 27*

**222.**_____

I'll be patient with any of your
insecurities as long as I see that
you're trying to overcome them.

*--Jason, 22*

## 223.

I've got to have enough light to see your body.

*--Dennis, 25*

## 224.

Any make-up is too much.

*--Fredrick, 30*

## 225.

Instead of telling me I need to shave before we make love, my wife will get the blade and cream and shave me herself. She's a rare and wonderful woman.

*--Ron, 37*

## 226._____

Once, we acted out a fantasy where I pretended to be the postman and she gave me oral sex through the mail slot in our front door.

*--Charlie, 43*

## 227._____

I love it when she makes these humming noises while she's going down on me.

*--Drew, 27*

## 228._____

Ask me to paint your nails.

*--Bruce, 29*

## 229.

If you ever get the opportunity to make love on a train, take it.

*--Tony, 28*

## 230.

Kinky is a very subjective term.

*--Gordon, 33*

## 231.

Before you get rid of any underthings, wear them one more time so I can rip them off of you.

*--Brad, 37*

## 232.

I know most guys would opt for quantity, but once you've had quality, you'll never go back.

*--Edward, 39*

## 233.

If you liked me enough to let me spend all my money on you, you should like me enough to go to bed.

*--Nick, 30*

## 234.

I don't care who you learned it from, I'm just happy you know it.

*--Austin, 26*

## 235.

The women I work with think I have my head down because I'm depressed. The truth is I'm checking out their legs.

*--Justin, 24*

## 236.

Fake hair, fake eyelashes, fake anything is totally unappealing.

*--Jefferson, 32*

## 237.

Every position isn't meant to induce orgasm.

*--David, 29*

**238.**_____

You can still be feminine without always leaving me wanting more.

*--James, 40*

**239.**_____

I love to feel your breath on the back of my neck.

*--Joseph, 35*

**240.**_____

Be competitive if we play a game together.  Hustle and spirit are big turn-ons.

*--Walt, 26*

## 241.

If there's a difference in your mind between romance and seduction, I need to know what it is.

*--Luke, 29*

## 242.

Let me know exactly what you want and what feels good.  When I'm guessing, nobody wins.

*--Bob, 27*

## 243.

Setting the pace and leading me on are not one in the same.

*--Earl, 42*

## 244.

Actions never speak louder than in the bedroom.

*--Kevin, 24*

## 245.

I've had enough of looking for your G-spot.

*--Anthony, 27*

## 246.

Always try to have something in the works (a weekend getaway, for example) that the two of you can look forward to.

*--Andrew, 30*

**247.**

I love to feel you under the table rubbing against my leg with your foot.

*--Larry, 32*

**248.**

Tell me about your first time.

*--Paul, 27*

**249.**

Every display of affection from me is not a request for sex.

*--Ronald, 31*

## 250.

Check you ego and your inhibitions at the bedroom door.

*--Danny, 28*

## 251.

We should spend more time just sitting around with no clothes on. You don't always have to be touching a woman's body to enjoy it.

*--Billy, 29*

## 252.

I'll try anything once.

*--Mark, 31*

## 253.

If it's been four days and you don't have a good reason (like you're on your period), something's wrong.

*--Matt, 26*

## 254.

I get turned on when my wife strips for me.

*--Ralph, 36*

## 255.

Allow me the pleasure of removing your bra and panties myself.

*--John, 29*

## 256.

We have our own interests and friends. We don't expect the other to like the same things in or out of bed. That keeps our sex life fresh.

*--Darren, 30*

## 257.

Oral sex on a vibrating bed.

*--Ted, 33*

## 258.

For the first couple of minutes of fellatio, only put the head of my penis in your mouth.

*--Jack, 39*

**259.**

Nothing personal, but I only use condoms I've bought. That way I know they haven't been tampered with.

*--Neil, 25*

**260.**

She's sexiest when she arches her back.

*--Phil, 29*

**261**

My favorite thing is to bury my face in her breasts.

*--Chuck, 29*

## 262._____

I like to watch her expression when she comes.  She's so beautiful.

*--Daniel, 34*

## 263._____

To get the most enjoyment out of receiving fellatio I have to be able to see you doing it.

*--Ricky, 27*

## 264._____

Please don't force me to stay all night.

*--Bryan, 30*

_____

## 265.

Suppressing yourself sexually because of other men means they still have control over you.

*--Mike, 39*

## 266.

Don't be afraid to touch my testicles.

*--Gene, 28*

## 267.

Sometimes when she's shaving her legs she'll cream me up and trim my pubes.

*--Dean, 29*

## 268.

Never put Ben-Gay or any of those creams on or anywhere near my penis or testicles. Not even as a joke.

*--Jon, 35*

## 269.

If I lost my job tomorrow, would you still do me with as much lust?

*--Stephen, 38*

## 270.

I like it when she takes off her shoes and she's four inches shorter.

*--Alan, 25*

**271.**

She's going to have an orgasm if it kills me.

*--Greg, 27*

**272.**

If she's fine and she knows it, I move on.

*--Bill, 30*

**273.**

I keep giving her foreplay until she begs for it inside her.

*--Phil, 29*

## 274.

Never stop flirting with me.

*--Steve, 31*

## 275.

The best sex you'll ever have with someone is after you break up with them.

*--George, 35*

## 276.

My wife doesn't feel like she has to prepare herself like a lot of women do before we make love.  That allows us to be more spontaneous.

*--Robert, 39*

## 277.

I don't have to be the first guy in your pants. This preoccupation with virgins isn't for me.

*--John, 28*

## 278.

I can't stand it when she just lays there.

*--Derick, 30*

## 279.

Take your panties in your hand and rub my testicles with them while you give me fellatio.

*--Ben, 37*

## 280.

Let's just take our time. No pressure.

*--Art, 31*

## 281.

Do it with both of you keeping your hands behind your back.

*--Scott, 34*

## 282.

The more animalistic, the more I like it.

*--Vincent, 26*

## 283.

Missionary with your legs on my shoulders.

*--Derrick, 29*

## 284.

I like just a hint of fragrance on a lady.

*--Norman, 40*

## 285.

I love it when I'm sitting up in bed and she's on top facing out.

*--Dave, 25*

## 286.

I love to feel her body on top of mine.

*--Patrick, 30*

## 287.

When the two of you are going to buy a recliner, get a good one that can support both your weight.

*--Keith, 33*

## 288.

If you're serious about wanting me to last longer, give me more foreplay.

*--Dan, 25*

**289.**

My wife doesn't tell me when she
wants to make love, she shows me.

*--Jim, 39*

**290.**

In order to get the perfect balance
of pleasure, take turns being selfish.

*--Ed, 48*

**291.**

My favorite is laying face down in
a rope hammock with my penis
sticking through and she's
underneath giving me oral sex.

*--Frankie, 31*

**292.**_____

I have this thing about feet. No monkey toes, strange bumps, or funky toenails.

*--Irv, 27*

**293.**_____

Some days I'll find a note in my wallet saying what she's going to do to me when I come home.

*--Mike, 37*

**294.**_____

It's the big mirror over the bed for me.

*--Craig, 31*

_____

**295.**

You shouldn't be jealous of the laughs I share with my buddies.

*--Larry, 25*

**296.**

Watch what my body does right before I reach orgasm. Once you know when to pull back, we can go all night.

*--Bobby, 23*

**297.**

When you talk, please have something to say.

*--Leonard, 30*

**298.**_____

Underarm hair on a woman is a
recipe for limpness.

*--William, 27*

**299.**_____

The sexiest thing about my wife is
that I know she'd love me
regardless of the size of my income
or my penis.

*--Mark, 32*

**300.**_____

An anklet is the sexiest piece of
jewelry a woman can wear.

*--Jeff, 30*

## 301.

The women on magazine covers are skeletons with skin. They do not define what beautiful is to me.

*--Karl, 38*

## 302.

It's okay to be bossy in bed.

*--Lewis, 26*

## 303.

The length of time it takes me to reach orgasm is not proportional to how much I love you.

*--Pat, 35*

## 304.

It's not what you wear, it's how you take it off.

*--Mathew, 29*

## 305.

A little razor stubble on her legs is sexy. Too smooth I feel like I'm doing a blow-up doll.

*--Geoff, 34*

## 306.

Sometimes we just make out like teenagers. When we get to the good stuff, we're ready to explode.

*--James, 38*

_____**307.**

I will never wait until we are
married before we sleep together.

*--Jim, 24*

_____**308.**

If you've ever been even slightly
curious about a threesome
involving another woman, please
let me know immediately.

*--Richard, 40*

_____**309.**

It doesn't matter what move you
make as long as it's the first one.

*--Erik, 29*

_____

## 310._____

You, me and a shower massage.

*--Frank, 34*

## 311._____

To a woman, the most threatening man is the one who knows she enjoys sex just as much as he does.

*--Michael, 32*

## 312._____

The key words are variety and frequency.

*--Doug, 27*

_____

## 313.

When we bathe together, always lather me up down there.

*--Lee, 28*

## 314.

Don't pierce anything but your ears.

*--Andy, 24*

## 315.

I love a woman who wants me to pin her arms down when we do it.

*--Joey, 30*

## 316._____

I love those little lines older
women get around their mouths.

*--Warren, 26*

## 317._____

We videotape ourselves and then
play it back adding play-by-play
commentary.

*--Donald, 32*

## 318._____

I don't like to be given directions
when I'm driving or when I'm in
bed.

*--Kyle, 25*

_____

**319.**

Don't french kiss me right after fellatio.

*--Thomas, 29*

**320.**

When you love each other, there's nothing too embarrassing to talk about or do.

*--Martin, 32*

**321.**

I love it when you can see a few stray hairs poking out of her bikini.

*--Kyle, 26*

## 322.

My girlfriend's period doesn't
bother me at all. In fact, I think she
gets into sex more when she has it.

*--Jamie, 27*

## 323.

I want to give you as many orgasms
as you can have, but you've got to
tell me what it takes.

*--Sid, 29*

## 324.

I'd love to find a woman who is
happy and satisfied with herself.

*--Robert, 41*

**325.**

I love watching X-rated videos with her. When they're doing it and you're doing it, it's like an orgy.

*--John, 34*

**326.**

We rotate who gets the remote control and who gets to call the shots in bed.

*--Chris, 28*

**327.**

Wear a long pearl necklace and climb on top of me.

*--Raymond, 29*

## 328.

I'm glad my wife keeps herself looking so good. No one should just let themselves go.

*--Earl, 52*

## 329.

Let me know when you're about to start menstruating so we can do it one last time.

*--Louis, 26*

## 330.

I really don't want to hear about your old boyfriends.

*--Reggie, 24*

## 331.

You would be amazed how much more I could love you if you loved yourself.

*--Ted, 34*

## 332.

I love a woman with a hearty appetite.

*--Mike, 39*

## 333.

When we discuss our sex life, how you say things is as important as what you say.

*--Bill, 30*

## 334._____

I'm okay with her cigarettes and she's okay with my beer. You give a little to get a little.

*--Tom, 32*

## 335._____

Get some fluorescent paint, color each other up and do it in front of a blacklight.

*--Randy, 26*

## 336._____

I like that she tells her friends what we do in bed. It keeps me creative.

*--Dan, 27*

**337.**

Stop asking me what I would do for
you in hypothetical situations.

*--Ken, 29*

**338.**

Imagine if we could only do it
when your nipples were hard and
how much pressure you'd be under
to keep them that way.

*--Parker, 25*

**339.**

Don't rate my orgasms based on
how much comes out.

*--Joel, 27*

**340.**_____

I like it when my girlfriend gets on top and leans over so her breasts brush against my chest.

*--Bert, 28*

**341.**_____

Let's both meet at home during our lunch hour for a quick midday lay.

*--Paul, 33*

**342.**_____

There are more women than men that thrive on problems.  Those are the ones I avoid.

*--Harold, 31*

_____

## 343.

Having some music in the background really helps to set a steady pace.

*--Todd, 33*

## 344.

When I take her to a fancy restaurant, I expect her to eat.

*--Stan, 28*

## 345.

I count getting undressed as part of foreplay.

*--Jerry, 29*

**346.**_____

Quiet girls are fine as long as they
pipe up during sex.

*--Rob, 32*

**347.**_____

Treat my testicles as gently as you
want me to treat your breasts.

*--Frank, 26*

**348.**_____

Fat or thin doesn't matter, as long as
the curves are there.

*--Michael, 34*

## 349.

Once, just for the hell of it, drink a bunch of tequila and shave your bush off.

*--Shawn, 27*

## 350.

I'm all for a romantic evening every so often, but you can't expect fireworks every single time.

*--Jeff, 30*

## 351.

Please do not pretend that you have or have not done something before.

*--Charles, 29*

## 352.

I could watch a woman work out for hours.

*--Don, 32*

## 353.

I still go to bars to meet women even though I'm not looking for a one night stand anymore.

*--Patrick, 30*

## 354.

I love it when my wife throws her legs over my shoulders.

*--Timothy, 28*

_____**355.**

Missionary with me standing and her on the kitchen table.

*--Jake, 30*

_____**356.**

Don't make me feel like you're doing me a favor.

*--Benjamin, 27*

_____**357.**

I love to kiss her breasts while we do it.

*--Anthony, 25*

_____

## 358.

You can use your teeth on my penis when I can use mine on your clitoris.

*--Dick, 27*

## 359.

The most flattering light to make love in is candlelight.

*--Nathan, 39*

## 360.

I hate it when the men jokes start flying and I'm the only guy there.

*--Arthur, 30*

## 361.

Run your fingers through my hair.

*--Don, 28*

## 362.

My wife has the most beautiful legs.  Part of why I love sixty-nine so much is because I get an unadulterated view of those gams.

*--Pete, 35*

## 363.

Do not bite or scratch me where every one else will be able to see.

*--Derek, 27*

## 364.

If a woman is too skinny I feel like I'm going to break her during sex.

*--Edward, 29*

## 365.

I love her curves when she lays on her side.

*--Bob, 31*

## 366.

You need to make the first move every now and then just to remind yourself how difficult it is.

*--Ethan, 23*

**367.**

Love only sustains the relationship
outside of the bedroom.

*--Bill, 31*

**368.**

We try to take a day off from work
together every couple of months.
While the kids are in school, we get
to do things without interruption.

*--Larry, 37*

**369.**

Sometimes I want sex just to take a
break from my problems.

*--Mitchell, 28*

## 370._____

I'd like to meet a girl who wants it at least twice a day.

*--Alexander, 24*

## 371._____

If I'm moaning, you're doing it right.

*--Carl, 29*

## 372._____

One of us, and it doesn't matter which, hanging in gravity boots.

*--Kevin, 27*

_____

**373.**

Never begin a sentence with, "If you really loved me you would..."

*--Tom, 30*

**374.**

Too much mascara makes you look like a raccoon.

*--Ed, 35*

**375.**

Nothing is more totally relaxing than strenuous sex in a hot tub.

*--Roger, 38*

**376.**_____

I prefer a woman who doesn't have to get emotionally attached before she can have an orgasm.

*--Scott, 30*

**377.**_____

I love it when we are finished and she puts on my shirt.

*--Keith, 36*

**378.**_____

She has to be ready and willing to experiment.

*--Adam, 27*

_____

**379.**

On your back with your feet on my chest.

*--Cliff, 31*

**380.**

Use the time you're away from each other to fantasize and then act them out when you're together again.

*--Dale, 37*

**381.**

I've got to be able to see it going inside you.

*--Tony, 24*

## 382.

Get your partner to videotape your lovemaking from their point of view. You'll learn a great deal.

*--Johnny, 26*

## 383.

Put your feet on my pelvis during missionary.

*--Ken, 30*

## 384.

Have a towel standing by.

*--Chet, 23*

**385.**

Stockings are a hundred times sexier than pantyhose.

*--Gary, 28*

**386.**

I like nice hands with nails that don't look like claws.

*--Robert, 26*

**387.**

I love it when she rubs my penis against her face.

*--Ron, 32*

# 388.

Don't be so close-minded about my previous experiences. You may learn something about yourself.

*--Philip, 29*

# 389.

My wife doesn't gossip to her friends about our sexual escapades.

*--Andy, 38*

# 390.

Oriental women know how to pamper a man. In return, they receive my unending loyalty.

*--Richard, 36*

**391.**

I'm not a mind-reader.

--*Dave, 27*

**392.**

My wife got a copy of *Playboy* and glued cut-out Polaroids of her head over the heads of all the playmates.

--*Matthew, 39*

**393.**

It's hard to be intimate with a woman who's hair smells like smoke.

--*Nick, 29*

**394.**_____

Decorate each other with cake icing
that you have to squeeze from one
of those bags.

--*Bruce, 23*

**395.**_____

Tease me while I'm driving.  It's
the next best thing to being tied up.

--*Mark, 28*

**396.**_____

Complete, total darkness forces you
to rely more on your other senses.

--*Jerome, 31*

_____

_____**397.**

I wish my wife would trust what her body is telling her during sex instead of her mind.

*--Rick, 36*

_____**398.**

I love it when she wears a big football jersey as a nightie.

*--Richard, 33*

_____**399.**

Sometimes my girlfriend "forgets" to wear panties.

*--Scott, 25*

_____

# 400._____

If you're constantly disappointed, you're expectations are probably too high.

*--Fred, 34*

# 401._____

The softer you touch my penis, the harder it's going to get.

*--John, 28*

# 402._____

Keep your waterbed filled to it's maximum capacity.

*--Bobby, 31*

_____

## 403.

Right after I've had an orgasm my penis needs some time to itself.

*--Robert, 30*

## 404.

I wish women didn't think sex was so "improper."  It's normal, natural, and can be quite pleasant.

*--Todd, 28*

## 405.

There shouldn't be a room in the house we haven't made it in.

*--Daniel, 33*

## 406.

Don't think of sex as a wifely duty.
It's one of many ways to share our
love.

*--Gregory, 36*

## 407.

You shouldn't need a drink to relax.
I'm a great lay even when you're
sober.

*--Alex, 25*

## 408.

Wash your car together, have some
fun with the hose, then get to it.

*--Gordon, 29*

**409.**

No matter what I do afterwards, I always feel like it's the absolute wrong thing.

*--Kurt, 23*

**410.**

Take your time when you undress.

*--Neal, 28*

**411.**

The best present I ever gave my wife was when I cut a hole in a box, wrapped it and stuck my penis in it.

*--Tim, 34*

**412.**_____

Accept that there are always going to
be women prettier than you, just
like there are always going to be
guys with a bigger penis than mine.

                *--Sonny, 26*

**413.**_____

The longer you keep it up before I
come, the longer it will stay up
afterwards.

                *--Ernie, 28*

**414.**_____

Crotchless panties.

                *--Anthony, 35*

_____

_____**415.**

Any part of your body that's warm feels great against my testicles.

*--Tim, 34*

_____**416.**

It's easier to be sexy than it is to be pretty.

*--Richard, 48*

_____**417.**

Just because we are in love doesn't mean we can't do it for the fun of it.

*--Peter, 26*

_____

## 418.

Angora sweaters.

*--Eddie, 31*

## 419.

I can tell when she does it because she feels obligated. I'd rather she respected us both enough not to.

*--Chuck, 34*

## 420.

The exhilaration you get from the danger of being caught in the act is nothing compared to actually being caught.

*--Ben, 39*

_____ **421.**

Tease me in a public place.

     *--James, 28*

_____ **422.**

I love all of your lips moist.

     *--Vic, 34*

_____ **423.**

I get aroused watching *her* watch the adult videos.

     *--Ken, 36*

_____

## 424.

Women most men would think of as gorgeous are too much work to keep happy.

*--Steven, 27*

## 425.

I love to watch her shave her legs.

*--Charlie, 31*

## 426.

I hope short skirts never go out of style.

*--Mike, 24*

## 427.

I can dish it out at least three times a day if she can take it.

*--Greg, 29*

## 428.

I'm very private. I expect my lovers to respect that and keep our experiences to themselves.

*--Nelson, 39*

## 429.

When I pay you a compliment, I'm not "just saying that"--especially if we've already slept together.

*--Dean, 32*

## 430.

I hate it when she compares me to her ex.

*--Laurence, 27*

## 431.

Let's try out different types of condoms.

*--Jeremy, 21*

## 432.

Start the day with some good sex.

*--Alan, 33*

**433.**

I tell you that I love you to get you in bed, you fake orgasm--they cancel each other out.

*--David, 27*

**434.**

I like the way my wife snuggles up to me.

*--Andrew, 30*

**435.**

If you come to my apartment and see a fire, a blanket and a bottle of wine--prepare to get laid.

*--Scott, 29*

**436.**_____

A sexy bra is nice.  No bra is better.

*--Rob, 34*

**437.**_____

When a girl has got in an IUD, I swear I can feel it poking me.

*--John, 31*

**438.**_____

If a girl is obsessive about her body, she'll never be satisfied with herself or me.

*--Kenneth, 35*

_____

_____ **439.**

If you own a dildo, I don't want it anywhere near me.

*--Samuel, 32*

_____ **440.**

She needs some coaxing, but every now and then I get her to do a little "dance of the seven veils."

*--Ron, 38*

_____ **441.**

Do it where he works. Every time he passes that spot, he'll think of you.

*--Al, 44*

## 442.

Not all men have one-track minds.

*--Louis, 25*

## 443.

A truly sexy woman can give me an erection without ever touching my penis.

*--Matt, 30*

## 444.

I'm always on the lookout for that visible panty line.

*--William, 31*

## 445.

Sweet foods, like whipped cream, taste great mixed with the salt on your skin.

*--Ernest, 33*

## 446.

When my wife wakes up, she looks like a little girl.

*--Tom, 32*

## 447.

Mattresses with too much give to them rob men of much of the sensation of intercourse.

*--Mark, 28*

## 448.

Never tell me you faked it, whether it's true or not.

*--Clark, 26*

## 449.

The most popular position is the least amount of fun.  The missionaries can have it back.

*--Cameron, 23*

## 450.

I like it as intense as you can take it.

*--Donald, 33*

## 451.

That stuff about meeting women in supermarkets is crap. My fridge is full, but my bed's empty.

*--Chuck, 27*

## 452.

The best sex I ever had was with a woman who bent over and took it like a man.

*--Jim, 34*

## 453.

Your mind should only be on what we are doing right then.

*--Daniel, 29*

## 454.

I love it when my girlfriend dances
nude for me. I'd rather give her
my money than some stripper with
stretch marks.

*--Dennis, 28*

## 455.

Once I was with a woman who
licked my anus. Part of me liked it
and part of me didn't.

*--Gregg, 30*

## 456.

Limber up like in aerobics class.

*--Victor, 35*

**457.**

Edible panties--yes.

> --*Larry, 26*

**458.**

Be yourself.  You don't have to
pretend to impress me.

> --*Bruce, 34*

**459.**

My penis is part of me, not a rubber
sex toy.

> --*Glen, 28*

## 460.

I take my first dates out for ice cream. If she licks around and around the cone, we go to a really nice restaurant.

*--Ed, 25*

## 461.

Wrap the blankets around us like a cocoon.

*--Pete, 30*

## 462.

Push-up bras and the wheel--the two inventions we're most thankful for.

*--Steven, 26*

**463.**

I need some oral or hand stimulation between giving you cunnilingus and intercourse.

*--Harold, 32*

**464.**

My girl has to be my best friend.

*--Bobby, 29*

**465.**

Show me how fast you can use your tongue.

*--Marty, 34*

## 466.

I wish we had more time and fewer kids.

*--Christopher, 35*

## 467.

I love doing it right before we are going to meet our friends.

*--Mick, 27*

## 468.

Sometimes after dinner I'll challenge my wife to a game of "Strip Jeopardy." We're both naked in about thirty seconds.

*--Tony, 33*

**469.**

When I get back from a business trip, my wife knows I want to make love before I even unpack.

*--Karl, 38*

**470.**

Tell me what gets you hot. I'll be happy to oblige.

*--Richard, 32*

**471.**

I love a woman who puts a little perfume between her legs.

*--Mike, 30*

**472.**_____

I like a lady with lots of curves.

*--Mark, 28*

**473.**_____

Unzip my fly with your teeth.

*--Jeff, 27*

**474.**_____

My wife and I have our best
moments after the bills are paid.

*--Harvey, 39*

## 475.

Tease my penis with little flicks of your tongue before full-on fellatio.

*--Wil, 26*

## 476.

The best sex I ever had was with a female ejaculator.

*--Rob, 34*

## 477.

A great variation on missionary is to stick your legs straight up and cross them.

*--Cliff, 28*

## 478.

Making love is wonderful, but lust for lust's sake has it's advantages.

*--Clint, 25*

## 479.

During foreplay, suck on my fingers as if they were my penis.

*--John, 31*

## 480.

I adore the way she fondles my testicles while she gives me oral sex.

*--Colin, 34*

_____**481.**

One leg on my shoulder and one leg
down.

--- *John, 29*

_____**482.**

Forget about mirrors on the ceiling.
Try making love on top of one.

--- *Frank, 54*

_____**483.**

She looks incredible when she
dresses up in one of my suits.

--- *Kirk, 35*

_____

# 484.

The biggest insult I ever received
in bed was when she smoked while
I gave her cunnilingus.

*--Anthony, 30*

# 485.

I like positions were she can reach
in and play with my testicles while
I'm inside her.

*--Michael, 27*

# 486.

I stay away from women with more
than one cat.

*--Tim, 31*

## 487.

Being open-minded enough to try
new things doesn't make you a slut.

*--Tom, 27*

## 488.

What would possess a woman to
wear black nail polish?

*--Brad, 32*

## 489.

Every guy on TV is screwing around
on his wife. That's not real life and
that's certainly not me.

*--Chip, 33*

**490.**_____

I like watching her go down on me.

*--Jimmy, 23*

**491.**_____

When it comes to women, youth is no substitute for experience.

*--Elmer, 48*

**492.**_____

I love it when she has that towel wrapped around her after a shower. It's great how one flick of my wrist can reveal her entire body.

*--Andy, 27*

_____

## 493.

Most guys want virgins so they won't have anything to compare them to.

*--David, 31*

## 494.

Doggie-style rules.

*--Matthew, 25*

## 495.

My wife knows that we don't *give* each other orgasms.

*--Joseph, 34*

**496.**_____

I don't like the idea of being with someone who's "been around."

*--James, 31*

**497.**_____

The best I've ever had was when we did it in my old high school homeroom.

*--Charles, 36*

**498.**_____

As deep and as hard as you can.

*--Wayne, 23*

_____

_____**499.**

How do you expect me to stay turned on when you're always saying how fat you are?

*--Robert, 32*

_____**500.**

Tight jeans are the sexiest article of clothing a woman can wear.

*--Doug, 27*

_____**501.**

There's nothing sexier than fish-net stockings.

*--Gene, 29*

_____

## 502.

When my wife wears her "French Maid" outfit for me, she doesn't use her feather duster to clean.

*--Theodore, 35*

## 503.

I love it when she gargles before she swallows.

*--Wesley, 29*

## 504.

Quality can be just as important as quantity to a guy.

*--John, 26*

_____**505.**

Fill your mouth with cold champagne and keep it there while you go down on me.

*--Grady, 27*

_____**506.**

I love it when my girlfriend fools around with my ears.

*--Jordan, 22*

_____**507.**

A little perfume goes a long way.

*--Glen, 30*

_____

## 508.

I like for her to gently squeeze my balls when I come.

*--Bert, 28*

## 509.

Romance is fine as long as it's in addition to hot, uninhibited sex.

*--Nathaniel, 26*

## 510.

Frail women make me nervous. I don't want to have to worry about crushing her or anything.

*--Stephen, 33*

## 511.

I'll last longer if you stop when I ask you to.

*--Charles, 25*

## 512.

I only go out with girls who don't have a problem with my opening a door for them.

*--Mac, 32*

## 513.

On a cool night, we'll drive around until the hood is warm, then make love on top of it.

*--Don, 36*

**514.**_____

I want her to dress in a classy outfit with sleazy, sexy underwear underneath.

*--Edward, 35*

**515.**_____

I love it when you give me little instructions.

*--Darren, 30*

**516.**_____

Sex isn't all I want, but I admit it's up there on the list.

*--Richard, 24*

_____

## 517.

I don't give a damn if the neighbors can hear us.

*--Philip, 38*

## 518.

I love cut-off T-shirts where you can see a hint of the underside of her breasts.

*--Brian, 25*

## 519.

I love to smell you on me after we've made love.

*--Ross, 27*

## 520.

If you can't find time to make love,
you're not living.

*--Rob, 26*

## 521.

Afterwards, tell me what you liked
so I'll be sure and do it next time.

*--Dan, 25*

## 522.

I'm not turned on by women who
draw their eyebrows on.

*--Lance, 33*

**523.**

The quickest way to get me to send you flowers is to say you don't want any.

--*Stuart, 34*

**524.**

Doing it standing up isn't the most satisfying, but it is the most challenging.

--*Michael, 27*

**525.**

When we climb into bed, I'm not looking for love.

--*Mark, 25*

## 526._____

I love a woman secure enough to crack jokes in bed.

*--Sam, 41*

## 527._____

I'll pay for the condoms, but it turns me on to watch you pick them out.

*--Adam, 23*

## 528._____

Keep your eyes open when we kiss.

*--Patrick, 30*

_____

## 529.

I respect women who can hold their liquor.

*--Kurt, 31*

## 530.

Every time I touch a girl with breast implants I'm afraid I'm going to rupture one of them.

*--Andrew, 27*

## 531.

I can tell she's told her friends what we've done by how they look at me the next time I see them.

*--Albert, 25*

**532.**_____

Too much jewelry on anyone is
tacky.

*--Rick, 28*

**533.**_____

When you are on top, ease me in a
little at a time.

*--Mathew, 31*

**534.**_____

Either swallow or don't let me
come in your mouth.  Never spit it
out.

*--Anthony, 27*

_____

**535.**

Doggie-style is my favorite.  We don't have to look into each other's eyes.

*--Jeffrey, 33*

**536.**

Women are always more beautiful the next morning because they're not caked with make-up.

*--Kevin, 29*

**537.**

Plan your sex life with the same variety you plan our meals.

*--James, 36*

**538.**_____

I'm not perfect. I sure as hell don't want a girl who thinks *she* is.

*--Timothy, 26*

**539.**_____

If you want it in you when you're not that wet, you're going to have to show me the way.

*--Gary, 30*

**540.**_____

My wife uses my penis as a drink stirrer (except when we have company over).

*--Vincent, 29*

## 541.

I hate it when there's music on. I can't get into it unless I can hear our bodies.

*--Stan, 27*

## 542.

Big butts give you something to thrust against.

*--Neal, 24*

## 543.

No matter how tired I am, be persistent and I'll do it. Then I'll thank you for getting me to.

*--Bill, 38*

**544.**_____

I love it when she massages me
from head to toe.

*--Don, 25*

**545.**_____

You can ask for anything and I
promise I won't think you're
perverted.

*--Jim, 31*

**546.**_____

I love those stockings with the
little line running up the back.

*--Gregory, 34*

_____

_____**547.**

Tell me I look good naked.

*--Tom, 33*

_____**548.**

I'd like oral sex a lot more often--
getting and giving.

*--Scott, 28*

_____**549.**

Fellatio with me standing.

*--Paul, 32*

_____

**550.**_____

Sometimes let's forgo all the foreplay.

*--Mike, 25*

**551.**_____

I love for you to tell me what you're wearing underneath.

*--Henry, 28*

**552.**_____

If you can't tell me what you want, show me with your hand.

*--Joey, 34*

_____

## 553.

When we shower together, let me wash your pink parts.

*--Jon, 24*

## 554.

If she can do a split, I want to get to know her.

*--Rich, 33*

## 555.

Allow me to introduce you to my stiff, straight-backed chair.

*--Mort, 29*

**556.**_____

There is nothing better than when she wakes me up ready for sex.

*--Laurence, 36*

**557.**_____

I love it when she rubs my penis between her breasts.

*--Nick, 27*

**558.**_____

Keep your legs as close together as you can.  The tighter the better.

*--Arnold, 39*

_____

_____**559.**

Unzip me and take my penis out
without unbuttoning my pants.

*--Randy, 30*

_____**560.**

Accept my faults as I do yours.

*--James, 34*

_____**561.**

You're never going to know how
good sex can be until you trust me.

*--Ken, 31*

_____

## 562.

My wife and I were friends for a long time before we became romantically involved. It's made the difference.

*--Jack, 39*

## 563.

The signals women send us are always too subtle.

*--Lorne, 27*

## 564.

Have a nasty mouth in the bedroom.

*--Cal, 29*

## 565.

Nothing's better than coming home and finding you waiting for me in bed.

*--Mitch, 37*

## 566.

Sometimes the romance can come after the sex.

*--Evan, 28*

## 567.

Fingernails scratching my back are good; fingernails scratching my testicles are bad.

*--Eric, 25*

**568.**_____

I love it when she comes on to me.

*--Steve, 26*

**569.**_____

The best sex to me is when we give each other an orgasm with our hands, our mouths, then our genitals.

*--Scott, 30*

**570.**_____

Instead of going in and out all the time, try left to right.

*--Tucker, 37*

_____

**571.**

Explore my body with a mouthful of ice cream. You pick the flavor.

*--Rob, 34*

**572.**

I'm not opposed to good food, good wine, and good music just because I'm a man.

*--Pat, 35*

**573.**

I love doing it laying on our sides from behind.

*--Bob, 27*

**574.**_____

Women who really work for a
living, like waitresses, are the most
passionate and satisfying lays.

*--Paul, 38*

**575.**_____

We start on the table, then she wraps
her legs around me and I pick her
up.

*--Darryl, 26*

**576.**_____

If I know she can't get pregnant, I
can relax and enjoy.

*--Matt, 23*

## 577.

You should try it drifting on a small catamaran.

*--Kirk, 33*

## 578.

The women I enjoy spending time with most are comfortable with themselves in every way.

*--Edward, 36*

## 579.

I love it when she sucks on my tongue while we're kissing.

*--Ritchie, 25*

# 580.

When my wife initiates sex, instead of me always leading the way, I really feel like she wants me.

*--Jay, 33*

# 581.

I'm underneath her doing cunnilingus and she's holding a bunch of grapes next to her vagina. I take turns partaking of each.

*--Derrick, 31*

# 582.

Ask me questions about my body.

*--Peter, 28*

**583.**

We start with sixty-nine, me on the bottom, my legs off the edge of the bed. I put my arms around her waist and stand up. Now she's giving me fellatio upside-down.

*--Marty, 26*

**584.**

I love to feel her hair tickle my thighs.

*--John, 34*

**585.**

Foreplay isn't all for your benefit.

*--Thomas, 30*

## 586.

Start with my toes, and lick your way up.

*--Tony, 31*

## 587.

She has to be able to look into my eyes when she's giving me oral sex.

*--Dave, 26*

## 588.

Women claim they want guys who'll put them on a pedestal, but they never respect us when we do that.

*--Mark, 34*

**589.**

We have these massage balls with bumps on them that really make your body sensitive to the touch.

*--Manuel, 30*

**590.**

If you can't tell *me*, who can you tell?

*--Robert, 35*

**591.**

Don't ever give me a sympathy lay.

*--Kevin, 27*

**592.**_____

Button your blouse one button less
than you normally do.

*--Dennis, 32*

**593.**_____

I love it when she fondles her own
breasts while we make love.

*--Mike, 29*

**594.**_____

I get off on her getting off.

*--Victor, 33*

_____

## 595.

Counting foreplay and intercourse, you shouldn't spend more than half the time on your back.

*--Keith, 31*

## 596.

I hate it when my wife makes me feel like she's letting me "do my business."

*--Pete, 37*

## 597.

Mohawks aren't just for your head.

*--Cliff, 25*

**598.**

I love the way my girlfriend touches me everywhere.

*--Rodger, 26*

**599.**

If you're both going to smoke a cigarette after, share one.

*--Patrick, 34*

**600.**

My wife traces messages on my bare back with her fingers. It's relaxing to concentrate on what she's saying. It's always something dirty.

*--William, 31*

## 601.

Try to do or say something that will separate this time from all the others.

*--Matt, 29*

## 602.

Men think of sex as more of a stress reduction technique.

*--Neil, 31*

## 603.

When you're on top, alternate between leaning all the way forward and all the way back.

*--Dave, 35*

## 604.

A sexy woman is one who is on the pill.

*--Howard, 25*

## 605.

We always use a lubricant, but instead of lubing me up by hand she squirts some in her cleavage.

*--Lawrence, 30*

## 606.

It's easy to please a man.  Just be there and act like you like it.

*--Greg, 27*

**607.**

Nibble all around my ears.

*--Don, 27*

**608.**

The best sexual experience was with a college girl in her dorm, with her roommate sleeping just across the room.

*--Mark, 34*

**609.**

Once I dated a girl who wrote little instructions above each body part with a marker.

*--Frank, 38*

## 610.

Rub your breasts over every inch of me.

*--Ben, 33*

## 611.

Satisfying my animalistic sexual urges brings out other primitive urges like protecting and providing.

*--Joseph, 35*

## 612.

Play with my nipples more.

*--Lee, 27*

**613.**

My wife drives me crazy when she gets on top and slowly moves her pelvis in a circle.

*--Dan, 35*

**614.**

I like girls with soft heels.

*--Bobby, 24*

**615.**

Trace circles around my nipples with your tongue.

*--Dennis, 32*

# 616.

How can you not have time for sex? That's what we're all here for.

*--Wayne, 38*

# 617.

Find out my favorite dessert and then, one night, spread it all over your body.

*--Dale, 31*

# 618.

Take me into your mouth more often.

*--Mike, 27*

_____**619.**

Having a vasectomy doesn't make
me less of a man.

*--Norman, 39*

_____**620.**

The "nice girls" are always the ones
with the most checkered past.

*--Chris, 31*

_____**621.**

My girlfriend's favorite pastime is
putting my penis inside an empty
three-liter soda bottle and arousing
me to the point that I can't get it off.

*--Sean, 24*

**622.**_____

I love it when she gets so wet, I
slide right in.

       *--Craig, 25*

**623.**_____

I love to hold her hair like reins
when I do it from behind.

       *--James, 32*

**624.**_____

I'd rather have one girl a thousand
ways than a thousand girls the same
way.

       *--Ted, 30*

_____

## 625.

Humans are creatures of habit, so you have to make a conscious effort not to fall into a rut.

*--Robert, 32*

## 626.

Give me a woman in red. That's definitely the color of sex.

*--Paul, 31*

## 627.

My girlfriend likes it when I call one of those phone sex numbers and she can listen on the other line.

*--Scott, 28*

**628.**_____

It takes more to be special than
spelling your name some weird
way.

*--Andrew, 34*

**629.**_____

Believe me, if I could keep from
coming until you were completely
satisfied I would.

*--Adam, 25*

**630.**_____

Don't be shy about showing
yourself to me.

*--Dave, 30*

_____

## 631.

The best orgasms I've ever had have all been the result of fellatio.

*--Phil, 34*

## 632.

I love to be there when she takes her hair down or out of a ponytail and watch it cascade down to her shoulders.

*--Charles, 25*

## 633.

I don't want to smell perfume, I want to smell you.

*--Billy, 26*

**634.**_____

Just let me look at you.

*--Nick, 31*

**635.**_____

Put my head in your lap and
message my temples.

*--John, 36*

**636.**_____

I love to lick the arch of my wife's
foot.

*--Karl, 39*

_____

**637.**

I'm not going to keep asking you what you want like some kid at a fast food restaurant. Tell me.

*--Hank, 27*

**638.**

I love the way she presses my face into her breasts when we're just messing around.

*--Tom, 32*

**639.**

I get turned on seeing how other guys look at her when we're out.

*--Rick, 28*

## 640.

If you're going to bathe together, do a real bath instead of a shower.

*--Brian, 35*

## 641.

You should be with someone who makes you feel proud.

*--Danny, 27*

## 642.

Tight, leather skirts do the trick.

*--Frank, 30*

**643.**

Try not to be so uptight.

*--Steve, 23*

**644.**

I use her nipples as an arousal barometer.

*--Grant, 26*

**645.**

I love to have her sit on my lap while we watch television.

*--Mike, 33*

## 646.

I'm a firm believer in "lust at first sight," but you sell love short if you think it happens in an instant.

*--Tim, 35*

## 647.

Make love anywhere near the water and it will naturally be better.

*--Adam, 38*

## 648.

I love it when she licks her lips right before she kisses me.

*--Charlie, 27*

_____**649.**

Being sexy is a state of mind.

*--Douglas, 34*

_____**650.**

When she isn't afraid to be silly and playful, anything can happen.

*--Johnny, 27*

_____**651.**

Marital aids are crutches.

*--Mark, 29*

_____

## 652.

I know the girls that answer those 900 numbers aren't for real, but my orgasms sure are.

*--Scott, 30*

## 653.

The flashier the better.

*--Ben, 29*

## 654.

I've known women who think that being in love means knowing instinctively what the other likes in bed. It doesn't work that way.

*--Tom, 35*

**655.**

I like when she puts her arm in
mine when we walk into a place.

--*Alan, 37*

**656.**

If you're into faking orgasm, I'm
sure you won't mind if I give you a
fake diamond.

--*Bernard, 29*

**657.**

If you think you've done it all and
can't learn anything new, you're
wrong.

--*Wayne, 35*

## 658.

Tell me what you like about my
body.

*--Aaron, 23*

## 659.

Don't be ashamed of your body.

*--David, 30*

## 660.

I can't unscrew my penis and give it
to you for safekeeping, so you're
just going to have to learn to trust
me.

*--Jim, 39*

**661.**

Since we've been trying to have a baby, sex has become much more clinical and boring.

*--Steven, 33*

**662.**

My wife likes movies. I like the way she "borrows" from them to make me feel good.

*--George, 38*

**663.**

Press up against me hard when we slow dance.

*--Mike, 28*

## 664.

If I had been with more women before I got married, I think I'd be able to satisfy her more completely.

*--Pat, 32*

## 665.

Real breasts are far superior to those silicone jobs, even if they're not perfect.

*--Chuck, 42*

## 666.

Sex after a heated argument is great.

*--Ken, 31*

**667.**

If you don't know how to dance together, take lessons.

*--Tom, 37*

**668.**

I love to wake up with her in my arms.

*--Michael, 26*

**669.**

When I ejaculate, I like to watch it come out like in X-rated videos.

*--Ray, 40*

**670.**_____

You can't embarrass me when we're
alone.  Get crazy.

*--Glenn, 27*

**671.**_____

I think it's really hot when a girl
rubs my semen all over her body.

*--Louis, 24*

**672.**_____

Think of my navel as an erogenous
zone.

*--Alex, 28*

_____

**673.**

A woman needs to be able to express herself sexually without using words.

*--Joseph, 35*

**674.**

Give me oral sex only using your tongue.

*--Walter, 30*

**675.**

I don't see what's attractive about a man's body.  That's why I need to hear it from her.

*--Bob, 27*

**676.**_____

My biggest turn-off is when she
tries to catch me in a lie.

*--Vincent, 33*

**677.**_____

I need at least a half an hour before I
can get it up again. Be patient.

*--Bruce, 30*

**678.**_____

Every woman should have a pair of
boxer shorts.

*--Daniel, 25*

_____**679.**

I get off on the way my girlfriend
nips at my butt.

*--Todd, 23*

_____**680.**

I love it when she takes my shoes
off for me.

*--Hal, 34*

_____**681.**

Please don't keep a tissue or hanky
in your cleavage.

*--Reg, 27*

_____

## 682.

A woman shouldn't have to spend more than ten minutes to get ready for anything.

*--Peter, 27*

## 683.

We've been together long enough to learn to be inventive. Sometimes we'll pick each other up in a bar and have a "one night stand."

*--Rob, 38*

## 684.

Long hair makes any woman sexier.

*--Al, 25*

## 685.

I would love some reassurance after sex.

*--Donnie, 25*

## 686.

I can't stand a woman who wears those old lady, orthopedic-looking shoes.

*--Butch, 36*

## 687.

If you're wearing a dress with a zipper in the back, always ask me to unzip you.

*--Timothy, 30*

**688.**_____

It's fun to be seduced by the woman
you love.

*--Christopher, 27*

**689.**_____

Use both hands on me during
manual stimulation.

*--Martin, 32*

**690.**_____

I love blouses that are thin enough
to show just a hint of nipple.

*--Jack, 37*

_____

**691.**

I love it when women enjoy getting oral sex, because I really enjoy giving it.

*--Tom, 29*

**692.**

Have sex in a barn and act like animals.

*--John, 31*

**693.**

It's okay to be sleazy with the person you love.

*--Mark, 29*

**694.**_____

No excessive body hair.

                    *--Phillip, 28*

**695.**_____

I love it when I'm sleeping and she
reaches over and helps herself.

                    *--Frank, 34*

**696.**_____

Oral sex, on men or women, is an
acquired taste.  If you don't like it,
or your man doesn't like it, just
give it more time.

                    *--Justin, 21*

_____

## 697.

The one thing I absolutely love is when my girlfriend walks up behind me, reaches around and plays with my penis.

*--Jeff, 31*

## 698.

Girls who take charge are turn-ons.

*--Gregory, 33*

## 699.

My wife's idea of making the first move is to suggest we have oysters for dinner.

*--Steve, 30*

**700.**_____

Every fall, we rake up a big pile of
leaves, throw a blanket on top of
them and make great love.

*--Dick, 45*

**701.**_____

When I'm stressed out I just want an
orgasm and to be left alone.

*--Johnathan, 38*

**702.**_____

Putting a pillow under your butt
makes a big difference in how good
it feels.

*--Perry, 29*

**703.**

The best thing about one night
stands is that you'll never see each
other again, so you can do whatever
you want.

*--Larry, 30*

**704.**

If her eyebrows are thicker than
mine, no way.

*--Ben, 25*

**705.**

On a private beach with plenty of
suntan oil.

*--Jerry, 31*

# 706.

There is a difference between
vanity and confidence.  I prefer the
latter.

*--Carl, 37*

# 707.

I've never understood why some
women feel guilty after sex.  Is
there something I should know
about?

*--Dave, 35*

# 708.

She's got to want it, too.

*--Jeffrey, 35*

## 709.

My most memorable experience involved this long-haired girl. She wrapped her hair around my penis and then got me off with her hands.

*--Wendell, 32*

## 710.

When you're on top, make sure you don't raise up so high my penis comes out.

*--Paul, 26*

## 711.

Nude Twister.

*--Tom, 33*

## 712.

I look for women with some
individuality.

*--Jerome, 30*

## 713.

If you want me to tell you what I
want, make me feel comfortable and
confident.

*--Garry, 27*

## 714.

Contrary to popular belief, I'm not
looking for a cook, a maid, or a
mother.

*--Mike, 34*

**715.**

My wife rented a limo.  We made
love in it while the driver took us
around and around our block.

*--Chad, 30*

**716.**

I'd like to be with someone who
could show me something new.

*--Hal, 36*

**717.**

What I do to earn a living doesn't
define who I am as a person.

*--Lawrence, 39*

## 718.

I like outgoing women who put others at ease.

*--Richard, 32*

## 719.

My wife and I went to a drive-in movie for the first time in years. We hadn't forgotten how to steam up those windows.

*--Ed, 45*

## 720.

Women love it when I floss with one of their pubic hairs.

*--Jackie, 25*

_____**721.**

Try everything once.  Do the things
you like twice.

   *--Jon, 29*

_____**722.**

I don't care for all the mind games
so many women like to play.

   *--Doug, 34*

_____**723.**

There's nothing more beautiful than
a woman's flushed face after an
orgasm.

   *--Bryan, 31*

_____

**724.**_____

No matter how slow you think
you're going, go slower.

*--Pat, 38*

**725.**_____

Part of the excitement is not
knowing what might happen next.

*--Kyle, 26*

**726.**_____

I like a girl who can take all of me.

*--Elliot, 29*

_____

**727.**

Independent, intelligent women with their own goals and desires are most attractive.

*--George, 40*

**728.**

A soft, sexy laugh makes me crazy.

*--Steve, 27*

**729.**

On our anniversary, I rented a bubble machine from a party supply store. You can't help but have fun surrounded in bubbles.

*--Matt, 25*

# 730.

Those short tops that showed the belly need to come back in style.

*--Larry, 39*

# 731.

I'm no god, but she makes me feel like one.

*--Scott, 30*

# 732.

Try it in an outdoor hot tub in the middle of winter.

*--James, 34*

_____**733.**

For my birthday, my wife knitted
me a penis cozy.

*--John, 30*

_____**734.**

Women are under too much
pressure to look youthful.  Age adds
character and appeal to a woman just
like it does to a man.

*--Todd, 25*

_____**735.**

I have a problem with belly buttons
that aren't "innies."

*--Andy, 31*

_____

## 736.

The best sex is the kind where you're so into it, you start slapping and slamming each other.

*--Dave, 32*

## 737.

It's sexy the way her panties ride up her ass.

*--Michael, 35*

## 738.

I love it when my wife gets on top and moves from side to side.

*--Christian, 27*

**739.**

Don't act so damned pristine.

*--Chuck, 28*

**740.**

The most unusual place was on a hayride under the hay with lots of people around. Nobody knew but us.

*--William, 29*

**741.**

Sex isn't good unless you use your mind, too.

*--Timothy, 35*

**742.**_____

I shouldn't have to keep telling you
that I love you every five minutes.

*--Tommy, 25*

**743.**_____

I love those rare occasions when I
get a cat-call or a whistle.

*--Ian, 38*

**744.**_____

When you don't expect sex and you
get sex, it's like winning the nookie
lottery.

*--Don, 35*

**745.**

Be the one in charge.

*--Mel, 36*

**746.**

She always has on a flavored lip gloss. Whenever I kiss her she tastes like a different candy.

*--Sam, 29*

**747.**

I want a woman who can be my playmate, my friend, and my lover.

*--Alan, 35*

**748.**_____

The only present I ever want for my
birthday is for you to be my sex
slave for the day.

*--Richard, 33*

**749.**_____

It cracks me up when my wife
makes up one of her special songs
about me.

*--Vincent, 30*

**750.**_____

I don't like know-it-alls.

*--Brent, 27*

_____

**751.**

Tickle me.

*--Pete, 29*

**752.**

I was up on the roof making some repairs. My wife climbed up to bring me a few tools, and somehow we ended up making love. We're still trying to top that one.

*--Thomas, 38*

**753.**

A good pillow fight works wonders.

*--Rick, 31*

## 754.

Fantasy is fine. The reality is that I love my wife, and not all men are unfaithful.

*--Randy, 34*

## 755.

I love smelling her perfume on me after we've been together.

*--Neil, 30*

## 756.

Low maintenance women are far superior.

*--Stephen, 35*

_____**757.**

Do it on a trampoline.

*--Gary, 24*

_____**758.**

The sexiest outfit she can wear is nothing.

*--Freddie, 26*

_____**759.**

I love it when she's not the least bit hesitant about what she wants.

*--Nicholas, 35*

_____

## 760.

If you're not interested, say so.
Nothing ticks me off more than a
girl who gives me a fake phone
number.

*--Jordan, 21*

## 761.

If she bleaches her hair, she'd better
bleach *all* her hair.

*--Mike, 29*

## 762.

I hate it when my girlfriend refers
to my semen as "a mess."

*--Rob, 31*

_____**763.**

I like to put my penis between her breasts and get off that way.

--*Kenneth, 28*

_____**764.**

I love to hear her moan when she climaxes.

--*Jake, 27*

_____**765.**

After we make love, we give each other an alcohol rub-down.

--*Mark, 30*

## 766.

My wife and I made love in the kids' treehouse while they were at summer camp.

*--Andrew, 34*

## 767.

Take off some of that lipstick before you start kissing me.

*--Darryl, 26*

## 768.

If you don't want us to notice you, then don't dress that way.

*--Craig, 23*

**769.**

I like watching her getting herself off.

*--Joe, 32*

**770.**

The ultimate ego trip is taking your partner to a state of complete satisfaction.

*--Phillip, 33*

**771.**

The party shouldn't end once the marriage begins.

*--Tim, 28*

**772.**_____

I like it when she undresses me.

*--David, 25*

**773.**_____

When we go out to dinner with
friends, she fondles me under the
table.

*--Kirk, 34*

**774.**_____

Having sex in a place where you
shouldn't makes it a lot more
exciting.

*--Dan, 38*

_____

**775.**

Don't tell me you accept my apology when you really don't mean it.

*--Mitch, 35*

**776.**

Bathe together and paint each other with soap crayons.

*--Patrick, 34*

**777.**

The honeymoon is over when she starts farting in front of you.

*--Bob, 27*

**778.**_____

Suck on my fingers.

>                        *--Curtis, 30*

**779.**_____

The best sex I ever had was a one
night stand with a woman in the
fold out trunk of her car.

>                        *--Lenox, 30*

**780.**_____

Take it as a compliment that I want
to go to sleep afterwards.

>                        *--Bill, 27*

_____

## 781.

My wife takes our daughter's Ken doll clothes and dresses my penis up in little outfits.

*--Scott, 33*

## 782.

I need to hear the same things you do.

*--Art, 34*

## 783.

I love rubbing her vaginal juices all over me.

*--Erik, 27*

# 784.

Whenever I start becoming angry
because she's getting her period, I
always remind myself that it could
be worse--she could be pregnant.

*--Jeff, 29*

# 785.

I'm not a phone sex regular, but it is
fun to break up the monotony.
*--Dave, 34*

# 786.

Bend over and show it to me. That
will get any real man in the mood.

*--Mark, 27*

_____**787.**

Do it every way you can think of.

*--Dan, 28*

_____**788.**

My wife and I use blindfolds to encourage touching, exploring and trust.

*--Douglas, 37*

_____**789.**

"Horny" is a man's natural state. Nature intended it that way and only castration can change it.

*--Steven, 27*

_____

## 790.

Take my hand and make it do what you want it to do.

*--Rich, 27*

## 791.

After I come, I like to stay inside her until I get soft.

*--Sean, 30*

## 792.

My wife and I don't make love everyday, but we do show our affection for one another daily.

*--Michael, 38*

_____**793.**

I hate a passive partner.

>  --*James, 25*

_____**794.**

The one thing that's kept our sex
life good over the years has been
the flirting we've done with each
other.

>  --*Donald, 49*

_____**795.**

My wife and I tell each other our
fantasies, then act them out.

>  --*Bobby, 29*

_____

## 796.

Making love is more than sex and making babies.

*--Joseph, 32*

## 797.

I would love to just be able to lay there sometimes, too.

*--Jim, 27*

## 798.

Unless it hurts, why not give it a shot?

*--Edward, 26*

## 799.

Don't just videotape your sex.
Make a real short film complete
with a story and costumes.

*--Martin, 29*

## 800.

We have a Polaroid camera so we
can take sexy pictures and watch
them develop.

*--Ken, 35*

## 801.

Don't be shy about getting to know
my body.

*--Bo, 25*

# 802.

Let's make love now, not later.

*--Ricky, 26*

# 803.

When I went out of town, I found one stiletto heel in my suitcase. Along with it was a note telling me she had the other and was going to wear them for me when I got home.

*--Lance, 37*

# 804.

I love to feel her touch even when we aren't making love.

*--Robert, 39*

**805.**

Tell me I'm good at what I do.

*--Ray, 25*

**806.**

Just because we are different doesn't make one of us right and the other wrong.

*--Paul, 31*

**807.**

I love seeing her in things I bought for her.

*--Phillip, 34*

**808.**_____

Let me take your clothes off for
you.

*--Mike, 28*

**809.**_____

After I've had an orgasm, put your
thumb under the head of my penis
and squeeze out that last little drop.

*--Nick, 37*

**810.**_____

My favorite way to make love is in
a chair with my wife straddling my
lap.

*--John, 33*

_____

## 811.

A cue ball is very cold, very smooth, and can be very stimulating when rolled around sensitive areas.

*--Ernest, 28*

## 812.

Give me a chance to savor my orgasm.

*--Gregory, 41*

## 813.

My wife lifts up her skirt and flashes me when nobody's looking.

*--John, 32*

# 814.

After I've come I really want to get that condom off of me as soon as humanly possible.

*--Glen, 31*

# 815.

Practice fellatio on a peeled banana.

*--Thomas, 30*

# 816.

Shaving a lot of your bikini line gives me a rash on my face if I give you cunnilingus.

*--Stewart, 40*

## 817.

I had my wife make me a little card with her clothing and jewelry sizes on it so if I see something for her I'll know if it will fit.

*--Bradley, 36*

## 818.

When she puts on this mask of skin cream every night I feel like she's doing it to keep me away from her.

*--Mike, 34*

## 819.

I like to watch girls put on lipstick.

*--Dean, 23*

## 820._____

I'm not saying that my needs should come before hers, but they should be a very close second.  Before her family's and before her friends.

*--Arthur, 34*

## 821._____

Obligatory sex is almost as bad as no sex at all.  Almost.

*--Gene, 30*

## 822._____

Tomboys were great when I was a kid, but now I want femininity.

*--Charles, 27*

**823.**

Please don't mention the kids, housework or the PTA when we're doing it.

*--Albert, 37*

**824.**

Hairy toes are disgusting.

*--Stan, 25*

**825.**

Treat me the way you like to be treated.

*--Darren, 30*

## 826.

Women wear hose too often.  Bare legs are sexier than even the kinkiest stockings.

*--Russell, 30*

## 827.

Don't ever compare my sexual abilities to those of your ex-husband.

*--Jim, 32*

## 828.

I'm interested in any woman who can beat me at anything athletic.

*--Scott, 39*

**829.**

Too much hairspray and mousse is disgusting.

*--Alec, 31*

**830.**

I love it when she presses her whole body up against my back.

*--Brian, 29*

**831.**

Your jokes about how quick I reach orgasm are actually very hurtful. It's my fault, though, for laughing along.

*--Walter, 26*

# 832.

Doing it to rock or rap is so obvious.  Put on some classical every now and then.

*--Jonathan, 34*

# 833.

Most natural beauty comes from your attitude and outlook on life.

*--Mark, 28*

# 834.

Ladies, getting the dishes done isn't nearly as important as making love with your man.

*--Matthew, 45*

## 835.

Women in hats intrigue me.

*--Rob, 34*

## 836.

I can't help but think of how the
events in your life affect me
sexually.

*--Nick, 25*

## 837.

For my birthday, she dressed up
like a geisha girl and waited on me
hand and foot.

*--Mike, 35*

## 838._____

Wear cowboy boots and a hat to bed,
and ride 'em, cowgirl.

*--Clay, 29*

## 839._____

I just watch the way she moves and
I'm ready.

*--Sean, 26*

## 840._____

The most sensuous sex you'll ever
have involves you, your partner and
a little jar of honey.

*--James, 33*

_____

_____**841.**

Wear a pair of long white gloves
and nothing else.

*--Andy, 28*

_____**842.**

I love to watch myself move in and
out of her.

*--Joe, 25*

_____**843.**

She appreciates wildflowers as
much as a dozen fancy roses.

*--Bill, 39*

_____

## 844.

Women taste best right after they've completed their cycle.

*--Eddie, 27*

## 845.

Keep your eyes open and enjoy it with me.

*--Ken, 30*

## 846.

The best is always when we want it so bad we start doing it before we're even undressed.

*--Nathan, 29*

**847.**

I like to hear the sounds when she's really wet.

*--Dave, 28*

**848.**

The worst thing in the world is when she gives you all the signs, signals, says yes, and then changes her mind.

*--Dan, 30*

**849.**

I get off watching her lick the salt off her margarita glass.

*--Steven, 27*

## 850.

Why do so many girls think they
have to make you jealous to keep
your interest?

*--Dale, 25*

## 851.

I would love to try peeling off her
stockings myself.

*--Chris, 32*

## 852.

When you show so much cleavage,
you have to expect us to take a
glance.

*--Scott, 30*

## 853.

I think my nastiest thoughts looking at you while you're asleep.

*--Richard, 36*

## 854.

I don't mind getting a compliment or two, either.

*--Bob, 40*

## 855.

The pleasure I get comes from what we do before I reach orgasm, not from the orgasm itself.

*--Thomas, 29*

## 856.

Use your workout tapes to come up with new positions.

*--Jeff, 27*

## 857.

I would never hit a woman, but there's something stimulating about inflicting a little pain during sex.

*--Ted, 31*

## 858.

My favorite word in her vocabulary is "ohgodimcoming."

*--Benjamin, 35*

**859.**

Have your first orgasm during foreplay, then any you have through intercourse are gravy.

*--Rick, 28*

**860.**

Women nowadays are too competitive. I don't even think *they* know what they're trying to prove.

*--Wes, 25*

**861.**

I'm tired of hearing she's tired.

*--Alan, 34*

**862.**_____

Only sleeping with rich guys is
merely economic natural selection.

*--Reginald, 38*

**863.**_____

I don't always have to be thrusting
in and out. It's nice to be inside her
and still.

*--Leonard, 32*

**864.**_____

Sex is more exciting when you
know someone is listening.

*--Jon, 27*

_____

## 865.

I like to sit Indian-style with her wrapped around me.

*--Don, 33*

## 866.

You don't have to be heavy into S&M to enjoy a little smack from a ping-pong paddle.

*--Tony, 29*

## 867.

Sometimes I feel like I'm just the guy who happens to be attached to this penis that she likes.

*--Tim, 31*

## 868.

The best sex I ever had was best because there was trust, monogamy, passion, and spontaneity.

*--Jim, 36*

## 869.

When you're standing naked in front of another person, you're revealing a lot more than flesh.

*--Glenn, 35*

## 870.

Too weird?  Too kinky?  Too bizarre?  There's no such thing.

*--Greg, 27*

## 871.

It's important not to let other people, family and friends, put us in adversarial roles.

*--Kenneth, 32*

## 872.

Monogamy is great as long as you can be creative and inventive.

*--Alexander, 30*

## 873.

Wild sex is my way of combating the business-like demeanor that's expected of me during the week.

*--Daniel, 37*

**874.**_____

Let your imagination come into
play.  Be silly and romantic.

*--Sam, 36*

**875.**_____

Women have the ultimate power
over men.  The best lovers are the
ones that don't exploit it.

*--Christopher, 33*

**876.**_____

Trust your partner or get one that
you can.

*--Phil, 29*

_____

## 877.

Copulation is programmed into a man's brain as top priority from the moment his gender is determined.

*--Bernard, 26*

## 878.

You shouldn't feel embarrassed or degraded giving fellatio. There's nothing wrong with making the guy you care about feel good.

*--Brooks, 35*

## 879.

Let me watch you douche.

*--Mark, 27*

**880.**_____

If that's what it takes, stimulate
yourself when we make love.

*--Peter, 29*

**881.**_____

The only way for a man to get laid
these days is to pretend he's looking
for a wife.

*--Andrew, 25*

**882.**_____

My wife lets me shave her legs and
bathe her. I enjoy taking care of her
that way.

*--Adam, 34*

_____

_____**883.**

**There are few things more erotic than toe sucking.**

*--Tom, 30*

_____**884.**

**It turns me on to come *on* her.**

*--Keith, 26*

_____**885.**

**I cannot truly relax during our lovemaking until you've come.**

*--Lenny, 29*

_____

## 886.

Charm me.  Flirt with me.  Tease me.

*--Philip, 41*

## 887.

My wife made a clay mold of my erect penis and used that to make plaster statues--"phallic figurines."

*--Luke, 36*

## 888.

My wife left me a videotape of herself masturbating before she went on a business trip.

*--Todd, 30*

**889.**

The smell of a woman when she's menstruating is sexier than any perfume.

*--Wayne, 34*

**890.**

I'm not that into sports. I watch it on TV because of the things you do to draw my attention away from it.

*--Kevin, 27*

**891.**

If you don't want an honest answer, don't ask.

*--Chris, 31*

**892.**_____

My girlfriend and I make love out
on my balcony.

*--Fredrick, 29*

**893.**_____

Once my wife came to bed with a
can of Silly String. It was the best.

*--Charlie, 32*

**894.**_____

My wife and I re-live our first time
together every year by going out to
the garage and doing it in the back
seat of the car.

*--Joe, 48*

_____

## 895.

Every guy likes it when you make up a nickname for his penis. For instance, mine is The Red October.

*--Lowell, 28*

## 896.

I think women get way too attached way too fast.

*--Randolph, 34*

## 897.

If you don't use your vibrator when we're together, I won't use my inflat-a-date.

*--Jeffrey, 30*

**898.** _____

What's all this about feeling like a kid again? When I was a kid, I didn't get laid.

*--Edward, 43*

**899.** _____

My favorite is doggie-style with my hands holding her breasts.

*--Nick, 30*

**900.** _____

Being open and close doesn't mean you have to lose your own identity.

*--Aaron, 29*

_____**901.**

Put your hands on my butt and pull
me in with each thrust.

*--Troy, 24*

_____**902.**

One night, we went to the park and
made love on a swing.

*--Dennis, 37*

_____**903.**

Don't be too quick to uncouple
when it's over.

*--Tom, 52*

_____

## 904._____

I don't want sex when it's convenient. I like to be more spontaneous than that.

*--Eric, 29*

## 905._____

The finer sense of control you have in your hands can make for the most intense orgasms I've ever had.

*--George, 30*

## 906._____

I respect the fact that my wife sometimes needs to say "no."

*--Paul, 35*

_____

**907.**

I wish she didn't have to go to the bathroom between foreplay and intercourse.

*--Jamie, 27*

**908.**

Jealousy is very unattractive.

*--Michael, 32*

**909.**

All women should know how to squeeze those muscles in their vagina. What a feeling.

*--Eric, 24*

# 910.

Put the same time and effort into your sex life as you do with other aspects of your life.

*--Joseph, 39*

# 911.

I don't know why men were given nipples, but it sure feels good when you bite them.

*--Herbert, 30*

# 912.

She can tell her friends what we do as long as she asks me first.

*--Stephen, 25*

**913.**

Having an unpredictable partner can help sustain the romantic intensity of a relationship indefinitely.

*--Tom, 38*

**914.**

We all want attention, and making love is the best way to get it.

*--Timothy, 32*

**915.**

Men who cheat are looking for variety. When you get variety from one person, it's easy to stay faithful.

*--Richard, 27*

## 916._____

When my wife changes her
hairstyle, I can't wait to make love.
It's like I'm cheating on her.

*--Earl, 40*

## 917._____

I get more pleasure out of pleasing
her than I do from my orgasms.

*--Jack, 24*

## 918._____

No orgasm in the world could feel
good enough to throw away
everything I have with my wife.

*--Dirk, 26*

**919.**

She knows what I like. When she refuses to do it I feel she's turning our love life into a power play.

*--Bill, 29*

**920.**

There's nothing like being fondled on a ferris wheel.

*--Red, 27*

**921.**

Play with it gently afterwards and it will get erect again and stay up even longer.

*--Tracy, 32*

## 922.

Right before I come, stick your finger in my anus.

*--Tony, 27*

## 923.

The term "brass balls" is merely an expression. They're actually very, very delicate. Treat them as such.

*--Steven, 24*

## 924.

Sex toys are okay every once in awhile. If we used them all the time I'd feel like a third wheel.

*--Bob, 30*

## 925.

I love to kiss a woman after she's given me oral sex and swallowed. It's a great way to finish up.

*--John, 40*

## 926.

She's a great listener. I can get it all off my chest and then proceed to the sexual festivities.

*--John, 35*

## 927.

Men have feelings and a heart, too.

*--Bob, 27*

## 928.

I despise it when she calls me up just to bitch at me.

*--Don, 27*

## 929.

I wish she didn't always expect me to instantaneously be in the mood.

*--Chuck, 29*

## 930.

Don't underestimate the power of great smelling hair.

*--Leo, 30*

## 931.

Nothing gives me more happiness
and self-confidence that when she
initiates our lovemaking.

*--Arthur, 32*

## 932.

I love it when we come together.

*--Andrew, 31*

## 933.

I hate it when she starts and then
decides to quit.

*--Tim, 22*

**934.**_____

Try things you see in movies, then
add your own twist.

*--TJ, 27*

**935.**_____

Sex and making love are two
different activities.  And there is a
time for both.

*--Derek, 27*

**936.**_____

She drives me insane when she
licks the backs of my thighs.

*--Steve, 25*

**937.**

Nobody makes love politely and means it.  If you do that, I know you're holding back.

*--Doug, 28*

**938.**

Whatever I'm doing at the time, sex is always a welcome interruption.

*--John, 33*

**939.**

Sex is not a way to repay your debts or exact revenge.

*--Calvin, 31*

## 940._____

All men love the feeling of
conquest they get from sex.

*--Stu, 29*

## 941._____

More women should wear slips.

*--Manny, 32*

## 942._____

The head of my penis is the most
sensitive part of my body.  Feel
free to give it extra-special
attention.

*--Curt, 32*

## 943.

We share duties in the kitchen. We should share duties in the bedroom.

*--Jeff, 31*

## 944.

Once you've done it on satin sheets you'll never go back to cotton.

*--Robert, 39*

## 945.

I love it when she doesn't just undress me, she caresses my clothes off.

*--Jody, 26*

**946.**_____

Freckles on a woman's breasts are sexy.

*--Mike, 21*

**947.**_____

I love it when she goes out of her way to do the things only I enjoy: watching football, fishing on the river and fellatio.

*--Michael, 25*

**948.**_____

I can't stand women who bite their nails down to the nubs.

*--Ron, 27*

_____

_____**949.**

Of course I imagine what your
friends would be like in bed.

*--Steve, 30*

_____**950.**

It isn't that the girls in men's
magazines are more beautiful. It's
just that they don't expect anything
from me.

*--Tommy, 30*

_____**951.**

No press-on nails.

*--Shawn, 37*

_____

## 952.

You can tie each other up and still give your partner the ability to get free. It's less intimidating that way.

*--Edmund, 28*

## 953.

Use an egg timer and take turns teasing each other in three-minute intervals.

*--Mark, 28*

## 954.

I think my wife looks sexier in my pajama top than in any of her things.

*--Greg, 35*

**955.**

Write down things you want the other to do, put them in a jar and play "sexual roulette."

*--Allen, 24*

**956.**

I love it when we kiss and she lifts up one foot.

*--Lee, 25*

**957.**

We give each other a coupon book with favors you can redeem during the month.

*--Doug, 29*

## 958.

I know I've satisfied her when her legs quiver if she tries to stand up.

*--Jim, 30*

## 959.

If you want me to continue the seduction, give me a sign that it's working.

*--Scott, 44*

## 960.

If you don't want it to get in your hair--swallow.

*--Neil, 25*

**961.**

Laughing in bed doesn't destroy the mood, it enhances it.

*--Timothy, 37*

**962.**

Consenting adults are limited only by their fears.

*--Anthony, 31*

**963.**

Act with decisiveness in and out of the bedroom.

*--Walt, 25*

## 964.

Use different techniques, not different partners.

*--John, 27*

## 965.

Our best sex was progressing up two flights of stairs compounded with the impending arrival of my two roommates.

*--David, 31*

## 966.

Be outrageous, and don't feel guilty.

*--Adam, 30*

## 967.

Take the time you spend talking with other women about sex and use it to talk with me.

*--Steve, 42*

## 968.

The best is on the back of a Harley.

*--Graham, 29*

## 969.

We have special nights when one of us is the total servant to the other. This includes the kitchen, the living room and the bedroom.

*--Paul, 36*

**970.**_____

Sex can only be great when you're with someone you trust completely.

*--Roy, 33*

**971.**_____

Take my hand and guide it to your vagina.

*--Hugh, 30*

**972.**_____

Every couple should have a "magic suitcase" filled with lotions, lubricants, toys and whatnot.

*--Jeffrey, 31*

_____

**973.**

Even though there are drastic differences in our bodies, what we want from each other is identical.

*--Bill, 23*

**974.**

A good lover will at least listen and consider the other's sexual desires.

*--Andy, 32*

**975.**

Don't go to bed angry or horny.

*--Kenny, 24*

## 976.

You can't really enjoy yourself unless you have a positive image of yourself and your body.

*--Thomas, 32*

## 977.

I love it when I can see a little bit of her bra peeking over her dress.

*--Michael, 24*

## 978.

When you can confide in each other, you can't help but be close.

*--James, 35*

**979.**

Play pool, tennis or any game with the winner getting to choose their favorite sexual favor as a reward.

*--David, 28*

**980.**

I don't always want to move it into the bedroom.

*--Paul, 32*

**981.**

The best orgasm I've ever had is the one I'm about to have.

*--Oliver, 37*

## 982.

She'll occasionally serve me
dinner wearing only an apron.

*--Richard, 34*

## 983.

Forget video. If you want
something really sexy make an
audio tape of the two of you and
listen to it in the car the next day.

*--Hal, 40*

## 984.

Slow and easy, then fast and
frenzied.

*--Jack, 27*

## 985.

You don't have to lie and say I've got a huge penis, but you could tell me what a perfect fit it is.

*--Chris, 25*

## 986.

More sex.  More often.  More places.

*--Theo, 27*

## 987.

Sight, sound, taste, touch and hearing--appeal to all five at once and the result is total fulfillment.

*--Mark, 30*

## 988.

We make sexual "wish lists" for each other every month. It keeps things popping.

*--Lawrence, 31*

## 989.

I shouldn't be able to smell your perfume from across the room.

*--Matthew, 26*

## 990.

I just don't see how you can love someone and not be having sex.

*--Rick, 27*

**991.**

When you're stimulating me with your hand, move it back and forth like you're opening a champagne bottle.

*--Simon, 35*

**992.**

If you respect yourself, you won't use sex to get the material things you want.

*--John, 33*

**993.**

Sex should be a win-win situation.

*--Joey, 24*

# 994.

I love it when she plays with the hair on my chest.

*--Tom, 29*

# 995.

Do something different one time out of ten. You'll still keep me guessing the other nine.

*--William, 34*

# 996.

If you have a private backyard, don't let it go to waste.

*--Edward, 35*

**997.**

The first time we do it, give me
your panties as a memento.

--*Erick, 25*

**998.**

The only time we have sex is at
night, right before bed. I'd like to
try an afternoon here and there.

--*James, 37*

**999.**

I'll never do it with the Home
Shopping Club on in the
background.

--*Christopher, 30*

# 1000._____

My penis is like your house plants--
give it some regular attention and
nurturing and it will continue to
grow and provide you with years of
enjoyment.

*--James, 41*

# 1001._____

Take responsibility for your own
pleasure.

*--Ben, 35*

# What's YOUR Sex Secret?

Do you have a specific technique, insight or observation that every man or woman should know? If so, take part in this ongoing survey!

**1.** Call the *1001 Sex Secrets Research Line* at:

**1-800-398-1001**

**2.** A recorded message will ask for your FIRST NAME ONLY and your age.

**3.** When instructed, answer one or both of the following questions:

> **"What is the one thing you wish your partner knew about sex?"**

> **"Think back to the best sex you have ever had. What made that experience better than any other?"**

That's it. Remember, you're **COMPLETELY ANONYMOUS,** so don't be afraid to speak with total honesty. Thanks for your participation.